WRITER'S NOTEBOOK

D0521305

TELLING TALES

Writing Captivating Short Stories

by Rebecca Langston-George

CAPSTONE PRESS
a capstone imprint

Savvy Books are published by Capstone Press,
1710 Roe Crest Drive, North Mankato, Minnesota 56003
www.capstonepub.com

Library of Congress Cataloging-in-Publication Data
Langston-George, Rebecca, author.
  Telling tales : writing captivating short stories / by Rebecca
Langston-George.
      pages cm. -- (Savvy, Writer's Notebook)
  Includes bibliographical references and index.
  Summary: "Introduces and defines essential elements of writing short
stories accompanied by compelling writing prompts for practicing new
skills. Real-life author bios and excerpts enhance skills and
understanding"-- Provided by publisher.
  ISBN 978-1-4914-5991-1 (library binding)
  ISBN 978-1-4914-5995-9 (pbk)
  ISBN 978-1-4914-5999-7 (ebookpdf)
  1. English language--Composition and exercises--Juvenile literature. 2.
Creative writing--Juvenile literature.
  PE1408.L3185 2015
  808'.042--dc23
2015015332

Editorial Credits
Jeni Wittrock, editor; Veronica Scott, designer; Morgan Walters, media researcher;
Katy LaVigne, production specialist

Photo Credits
Capstone Studio: Karon Dubke, (book cover) bottom left 37; Getty Images: New York Daily News Archive, (walter) top right 37, Popperfoto, (Christie) top right 47; iStockphoto: duncan1890, 45; Shutterstock: Baronb, (sheep) top 14, Africa Studio, 31, africa924, top left 9, Aleks Melnik, (filmstrip) bottom left 22, bottom 34, Aless, 55, Alice Franz, 46, Aliona Manakova, design element, Annette Shaff, (chihuahua) bottom left 15, Areipa.lt, (milkyway) background 17, 18, Artography, (wall) background 39, Atelier Sommerland, (fortune teller) 18, BackgroundStore, top right 9, blue67design, 20, bluelela, 58, Canadapanda, (mall) middle right 29, chronicler, 30, 32, (old man) bottom left 41, chuhail, (book) bottom right 41, (magnify glass) bottom left 47, Cienpies Design, 19, Creative Travel Projects, bottom right 9, Daniel MR, (sticky note) throughout 14, 15, Eric Isselee, (dog) bottom right 11, Everett Historical, 59, Farferros, 5, Gil C, (alien) bottom left 16, hammett79, (zebra) middle left 15, Iancu Cristian, 28, Igor Zakowski, 54, ivangraphics, (robot) bottom right 17, janecat, (pigs) top left 15, Jearu, (lemur) middle right 15, Jennie Book, (ray) top right 16, KAMONRAT, (tiger) bottom left 14, KERIM, 25, Kobby Dagan, (band) top right 29, Leah-Anne Thompson, 8, lineartestpilot, 48, lyeyee, (girl images) 34, Macrovector, 49, 61, MANDY GODBEHEAR, (headphones) bottom left 36, (painter) middle 36, (reading) top 36, (sleeping)bottom right 36, marchello, (polar bear) bottom right 14, mayrum, background 7, meanep, bottom left 9 , milyana, 52, miya227, 60, mlorenz, (owl) middle 14, Nadalina, background 4, Natalia Skripko, 26, Nicram Sabod, (seal) bottom right 15, Nikiteev_Konstantin, (lightbulb) top 41, Oleksiy Mark, top right 10, (globe) bottom left 10, Pim, background 22, Rawpixel, 38, (bubbles) bottom 39, Robert Adrian Hillman, (headlines) background 11, rudall30, 51, SAHACHAT SANEHA, (lobster) top right 15, softRobot, 40, Syrytsyna Tetiana, 13, szefei, (girl) bottom left 42, 50, topform, (hipster) background 44, Tropinina Olga, (illustration) background 42, 43, v.s.anandhakrishna, 57, Vaju Ariel, 12

Printed in the United States of America in North Mankato, Minnesota.
052015   008823CGF15

TABLE OF CONTENTS

Introduction

Imagine the power you wield when writing a short story. By picking up a pen or opening your laptop, you can create new worlds, construct the future, or reinvent the past. In a short story, you can direct characters like actors on a stage. You can invent phrases and use language in new ways. When you write short stories, *you*, my friend, are in charge!

Are you ready to get started? Beginning your writing journey is easy. You'll discover how to tap your inspiration and plot like a pro. You'll breathe life into your characters and learn special techniques to create memorable short stories. Along the way you'll be mentored by famous writers and read the stories that earned them success.

Best of all, awesome writing prompts will kick-start your inspiration into high gear. Grab your pen and paper and let's get started.

Chapter 1

What Is a Short Story?

Like its cousin the novel, a short story is a work of fiction. It also has a plot, a theme, and a conflict. Short stories usually have one easy-to-follow plot rather than the complex, multi-layered plots found in novels. With a smaller cast of characters and a shorter length, a short story can be read in one sitting. While there is no set rule on a short story's length, typically short stories have fewer than 20 pages. Sometimes short stories are compiled into a collection. These collections might feature stories with a similar theme or stories using the same characters.

Reading short stories will help you become a better writer. Great writers are also great readers because they learn from example. Some of today's great short-story writers found inspiration from their peers, and you can too. Why not check out their work? You can read a short story in one sitting, so if you're serious about being a short story writer, make it your goal to read several a week.

Chapter 2

Get Inspired

What If?

Can you guess the number-one question authors are asked? It's "Where do you get your ideas?" The answer is easy—inspiration is everywhere! New ideas are just waiting to be discovered. The trick is to train yourself to look for inspiration around you. Asking questions often gets your creative juices flowing.

One way to get inspired is to ask "What if?" Washington Irving asks this question in his classic short story "Rip Van Winkle." Irving takes an everyday event, napping, and asks what would happen if a person didn't wake up from his nap for 20 years?

"On awakening he found himself on the green knoll from whence he had first seen the old man of the glen. He rubbed his eyes—it was a bright, sunny morning . . . 'Surely,' thought Rip, 'I have not slept here all night.' Upon returning to his home everything had changed. "It was with some difficulty that he found the way to his own house, which he approached with silent awe, expecting every moment to hear the shrill voice of Dame Van Winkle. He found the house gone to decay—the roof fallen in, the windows shattered, and the doors off the hinges. A half starved dog that looked like Wolf was sulking about it. Rip called him by name but the cur snarled, showed his teeth and passed on. This was an unkind cut indeed— 'My very own dog,' sighed poor Rip, 'has forgotten me.'"

YOUR TURN

Choose an everyday activity and ask yourself, "What if?" What if this task took a strange turn? Make a list of activities you do every day, such as brushing your teeth, eating breakfast, tying your shoes, or opening your school locker. Choose one action, and let your imagination run wild! What if your bowl of corn flakes made ears of corn sprout from your head? What if you reached into your locker for a book and a hand pulled you into a new world? Take 5–10 minutes and jot down as many ideas as possible. When you are finished, tuck away your list for a while. Come back to it later for story inspiration.

PLAN

Set Up a Great Story with Setting

Another great way to get inspired is to look at pictures of different places. The place and time where a story occurs is its setting, and looking at unique settings can spark story ideas. To get started, all you need are a few pictures and your curiosity. Try doing an Internet search for images or thumbing through old magazines for setting pictures. Pick pictures that appeal to you, such as places you'd like to travel to or places you've visited and loved. Look for settings that convey the tone or feel you want your story to have. For example, if you want to write a spooky story, choose images that have an eerie feel.

YOUR TURN

Choose the picture on this page that you find the most interesting, or find another picture of a place that intrigues you. Make a list of everything that could happen there. Don't be fooled by your preconceived ideas about the setting. Dig deep and consider what unexpected things might take place. What problem might have occurred here? Who or what might be lurking outside the picture frame? How has the scene changed from 100 years ago? What historical event might have happened here? What could happen in the future? Craft one to three paragraphs describing the picture's setting for use in a short story.

News Flash

Real-life stories happen around you every day. Your friends, family, and neighbors are all living out real-life dramas. The TV, movies, Internet, and newspapers are chock-full of reports of daily events. One way to create a great short story is to find inspiration in real life. Many authors use nonfiction events

and flesh out the details to create interesting pieces of fiction. Start carrying a journal, and write down bits and pieces of real-life events. Weave in some imagination, and you've got a story.

Watch the nightly news. Jot down notes on a story that interests you. Let the nonfictional news inspire a fictional story of your own. For example, let's say one of the news shows features a story about a dog that was lost for six months and suddenly showed up back at his house. His paws were worn and bloody, indicating he had walked a long distance. How did he become lost? How did he make his way home? What adventures did he have along the way? Invent the dog's story.

Why Board

In addition to asking "what if," authors also ask themselves "why?" Why are tears salty? Why do stars twinkle in the night sky? Stories that answer the question "why?" are called pourquoi tales. The word *pourquoi* is French for "why." Pourquoi stories are often about nature or natural occurences as experienced by human or animal characters. These stories are told through the voice of a storyteller. Look around the world at things that interest you and start asking why. Then let your imagination take over!

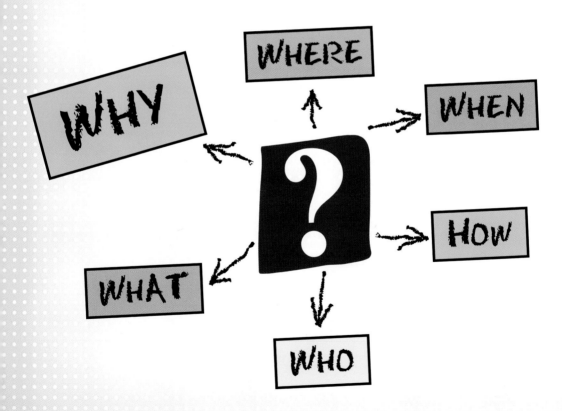

Getting to Know: Rudyard Kipling

Rudyard Kipling wrote a series of pourquoi tales called *Just So Stories.* One of his stories is called "How the Camel Got His Hump."

In the beginning when the world was new, a dog, a horse, and an ox all ask the camel to help with their work, but the lazy camel just says "humph." So the Djinn, or magical spirit, says to the camel,

"'What's this I hear of your doing no work, with the world so new-and-all?'

'Humph!' said the Camel.

The Djinn sat down, with his chin in his hand, and began to think a Great Magic, while the Camel looked at his own reflection in the pool of water.

'You've given the Three extra work ever since Monday morning, all on account of your 'scruciating idleness,' said the Djinn: and he went on thinking Magics, with his chin in his hand.

'Humph!' said the Camel.

'I shouldn't say that again if I were you,' said the Djinn: 'you might say it once too often. Bubbles, I want you to work.'

And the Camel said 'Humph!' again: but no sooner had he said it than he saw his back, that he was so proud of, puffing up and puffing up into a great big lolloping humph."

Create your own pourquoi tale to explain why something is the way it is. Animal pictures can help inspire your next amazing tale. Glue lots of animal pictures on a piece of poster board. Write down questions next to the pictures. Next to a lobster picture you could write, "How a lobster got his pincers." After you've put several animals and questions on your inspiration board, choose one and develop a story.

Write your iDea Here

Write your iDea Here

Write your iDea Here

Write your iDea Here

Write your idea here

How a lobster got his pincers.

Write your idea here

Write your idea here

Write your idea here

Write your idea here

AUTHOR PROFILE:

Ray Bradbury

Ray Bradbury made science fiction writing popular. His short story collection, *The Martian Chronicles*, is among his best-known works. In 1932 when Ray was 12 years old, he met a carnival magician named Mr. Electrico. Mr. Electrico touched Ray with his sword and proclaimed "Live forever!" This left a great impression on young Ray. Pehaps he thought he could live forever by leaving behind his stories. Right then and there, he started writing every day. He would later make it his goal to write at least 1,000 words a day. The author of more than 500 publications, Ray wrote, "The need to write, to create, coursed like blood through my body."

Science fiction is a popular genre—or specific type—of fiction. These highly creative tales are set in a believable but fictitious future. A science fiction story might take place on Earth, on a space ship, or even on a distant planet! They may features aliens, lifelike robots, or any other creature that the author can dream up.

It takes plenty of practice and talent to weave in futuristic elements without breaking the flow of a story. Remember, despite the fantastic marvels of science and technology, science fiction still must feel real and relatable on some level or readers lose interest. Every good writer knows that a story rooted in genuine human emotions and well-thought-out details can win readers' hearts. Sound fun? Want to give it a shot?

To try writing a science fiction story, why not take a classic fairy tale, like "Cinderella," for example, and rewrite the story in a future setting of your creation.

Maybe in your sci-fi story, Cinderella is a robotic technician who can't attend an intergalactic dance because she has to work. Even if she were able to attend, poor Cinderella certainly has no proper ballroom attire. Use your imagination to dream up her futuristic fairy godmother. What amazing transportation will shuttle her to the dance? Are her fantastic shoes heels or sneakers? Are they made of titanium or lunar crystals? Let your imagination play!

Chapter 3

Plot Your Course

Plotted Plans

Life is a chain or series of events and interactions—and so is a short story. Just as in real life, if you don't plan ahead, your story is going nowhere!

Story plots flow from the beginning to the middle and conclude with endings. In a short story, we call that the "progression of the plot." The progression of the plot is the thread that connects all elements of a story and keeps readers engaged.

If you break it down a little further, a plot has five basic parts. Exposition introduces the story's characters and setting. When a conflict, or problem, takes root and grows, it's called rising action. Climax is the point at which the conflict is at its height, and the scales tip toward change. The conflict drops off and things begin to return to normal during falling action. The last part is resolution, in which the conflict is solved. Although plotting takes a little time, in the end you'll find you saved time! A good plan will save you from staring off into space and wondering what happens next.

Visualize!

One way to plan your plot is to think of your story like a movie. First visualize the events that may play out in your story. Then sketch them out, storyboard style. To create a filmstrip, divide a long strip of paper into six boxes. The first box is your beginning, or exposition. The next two boxes are part of your middle, also known as rising action. The fourth box is your climax. Box number five is your falling action and box six shows the resolution, or ending. Use a pencil to sketch pictures of what will happen in each scene. Write down some words as well, if you like. Remember, you're creating a writing plan, not an art project, so try not to get distracted with colored pencils or markers. Once you've visualized your story and planned it out, the real fun begins!

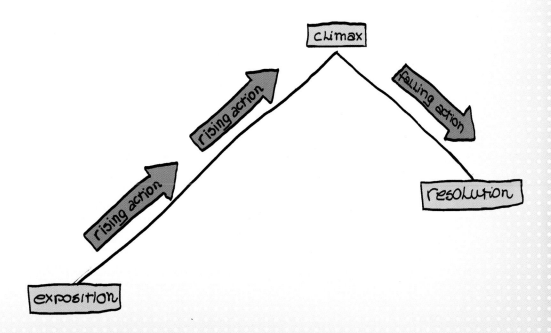

YOUR TURN

Need some inspiration? Get inspired by movie titles. Check your TV listings. Look at the list of old movie titles. Write down titles of movies that interest you. Use the storyboard visualization technique to form a plot based on the movie title of your choice. Now create your own story using the storyboard as a guide.

POPCORN

Conflict Drives the Story Forward

Conflict is a problem in the story that must be realized or overcome. WIthout conflict, a story is nothing more than a long description. When conflict is introduced, a story's gears start turning. Conflict can be a physical battle, a battle of wills, a fight for justice, or an emotional battle. Readers love to root for a character to win. Writers provide characters with conflicts to overcome so readers can sympathize and cheer them on. Conflict is the key to a great tale. All the world's problems boil down to four basic types of conflict:

CHARACTER VS. CHARACTER two characters struggle with one another	**CHARACTER VS. NATURE** nature is the enemy that a character must overcome
CHARACTER VS. SELF a character struggles against His or Her own feelings	**CHARACTER VS. SOCIETY** a character fights against an unjust society, government, or rule

Getting to Know: Jack London

Jack London is famous for his stories involving characters struggling against nature. In his short story "How to Build a Fire," a man builds a fire outdoors when it is 50 degrees below zero (-46 degrees Celsius). He has only minutes to light it before he freezes, but nature conspires against him.

"He should not have built the fire under the spruce tree. He should have built in the open. . . . High up in the tree one bough capsized its load of snow. This fell on the boughs beneath, capsizing them. . . . It grew like an avalanche, and it descended without warning upon the man and the fire, and the fire was blotted out! The man was shocked. It was as though he had just heard his own sentence of death."

YOUR TURN

Write a story in which nature is the enemy. Think of a situation in which someone would have to struggle to survive. An earthquake, flood, tornado, or avalanche might play a role in your story. Or a character could suffer hardships as a result of extreme heat, cold, or thirst. Make nature the villain that tests the limits of your character. Add some complications and pour on the drama. Your character's life is at stake. Will he or she survive? It's up to you.

Conflict Causes Characters to Change

Every story needs a conflict, but remember—not just any old conflict will do! A story's conflict has to serve a purpose and seem natural and believable within the story. It has to make a difference in the characters' lives and force them to face their problems. Have you ever heard the saying "What doesn't kill you makes you stronger?" Conflict pushes characters to the edge emotionally or physically. The conflict serves as a trial. Faced with difficult problems, characters are challenged and tested. They come out of the ordeal changed in some way, usually for the better. Conflict might cause characters to mature, be more compassionate, shift viewpoints, or understand things in a new light.

You've probably experienced conflict with other people in your life. Have you ever argued with a brother or sister? Do you always see eye to eye with your parents? Has a good friend ever disappointed you? These are all examples of character vs. character conflict. Any two people who spend time together on a regular basis are bound to have some conflict. Make a bubble map like the one shown. List all the relationships you have. Choose two characters from the bubble map and create a story about them in which a conflict arises. Think about how the conflict will make at least one of the characters change and grow by the end. Write your story.

Bubble Map:

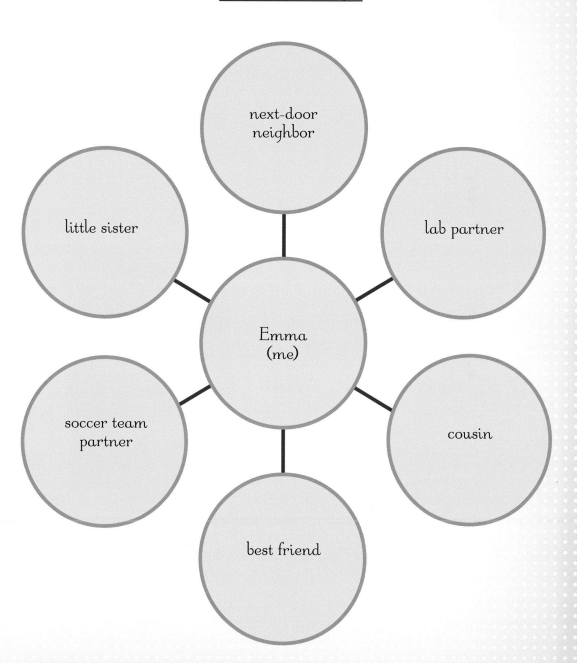

Make It Believable

Even with a great plot and an interesting conflict, a story can fall flat if it isn't believable. You want your reader to feel as though she has tumbled into your story world and is experiencing the action, not just reading about it. To create a world readers can get lost in, you need to infuse your story with vivid descriptions. Use specific, authentic details so your readers experience events along with the characters.

Let's take a look at two ways to describe eating a peach.

1. Maya ate a peach. It tasted very good.

2. Maya bit into the soft, golden peach. Velvety peach skin tickled the tip of her nose. Sweet, sticky juice trickled down the corner of her mouth, and she licked it up, not wanting to waste a single glorious drop.

Which is more interesting? The first one tells you what Maya does. The second one shows you what Maya does and uses lots of sensory detail. Think of your five senses—sight, hearing, smell, taste, and touch. In the second description the writer appeals to the readers' sense of sight, taste, and touch. Including sensory details will help your reader experience your story.

Describe something happening in one of these pictures. Include some sensory details such as how things look, feel, smell, sound, and taste. As you write, try to make your reader experience what is happening right along with the characters you create.

AUTHOR PROFILE:

Sandra Cisneros

Sandra Cisneros incorporates both Spanish and English words into her stories. Her writing shifts between the two languages so she can select just the right word. She feels the two languages give her twice as many words and meanings to select from and help her express herself. She is best known for her collection of coming-of-age stories in "The House on Mango Street." In it, Cisneros captures the everyday life of young Hispanic Americans. A former teacher, Cisneros has also created workshops for would-be writers. Her writing is characterized by unusual formats such as notes, overheard snippets of gossip, and poems.

Chapter 4

Breathe Life into Your Characters

Characters Have History

Imagine meeting someone new for the first time. Naturally you want to learn all about him or her—what kind of activities he or she enjoys, what you have in common, whether he or she is kind or brave or wacky. You're curious about your new friend's background and personality. When meeting a character in a great story, readers have a similar reaction. They want to know more. As a writer it's your job to deliver interesting characters that seem like genuine people. This is called characterization. The key to creating great characters is to treat them like real people with real-life histories. Think of it this way—if you're writing about a character who is 15 years old, that character has experienced 15 years of living before stepping in to your story. He or she has hopes, dreams, secrets, and fears. Writers call that a character's backstory. Use your character's backstory to create a seemingly real person who readers will relate to.

Imagine that your character keeps a special memory box. It is filled with things such as movie ticket stubs, photos, school play programs, notes from friends, certificates from school activities, and cards from holiday and birthday gifts. Write a diary entry in which your character describes the events surrounding one of these special items. Assume that your character has a vivid memory of the source of the item, so describe the experience thoroughly. What can you reveal about your character through physical description? Use your character's thoughts and actions to create a believable memory and history before the present.

Unique Qualities

In addition to thinking about your character's history, think about what makes your character unlike anyone else. What makes him or her stand out in a crowd? What qualities does he or she possess? Make a list of your character's personality traits. Is he or she brave? Untrustworthy? Kind? Generous? Now list some of your character's quirks, or peculiar habits. Maybe she's always late and out of breath. Perhaps he rides a unicycle everywhere. Does she insist on wearing high-top sneakers even to the prom? Generating character qualities and quirky traits will help you develop a believable, interesting character. Writers who skip these character development exercises sometimes find their characters are like cardboard cut-outs. They lack dimension and depth.

Getting to Know: O. Henry

O. Henry is famous for his surprise endings. One of his best-known stories, "The Gift of the Magi," is about two characters, James and Della Young. Della's pride and joy is her beautiful, silky long hair, which is the envy of everyone who sees it. James, though he is poor, treasures an expensive pocket watch he inherited. In the story's famous surprise ending, the two characters unknowingly sacrifice their favorite objects to buy one another gifts. By giving up the very things they treasure most, James and Della show how they value one another.

"Now there were two possessions of the James Dillingham Youngs in which they both took a mighty pride." One was Jim's gold watch that had been his father's and his grandfather's. The other was Della's hair. Unable to afford a Christmas gift for James, Della cuts and sells her hair to a wig maker. Upon coming home Christmas Eve James is shocked to see Della's short hair as he hands her a Christmas gift. She opens it. "There lay the combs—the set of combs side and back, that Della had worshipped for long in a Broadway window. Beautiful combs, pure tortoise shell, with jeweled rims—just the shade to wear in the beautiful vanished hair." Della then gives James the watch chain she purchased by selling her hair. "'Give me your watch,' she said. 'I want to see how they look together.' Instead of obeying, Jim tumbled down on the couch and put his hands under the back of his head and smiled. . . . 'I sold the watch to get the money to buy your combs.'"

YOUR TURN

Pick an item from the treasure box. Tell a story of the person who treasures this item and describe how it became so important in that person's life. Then imagine a plot or sequence of events that would cause the character to part with the object.

Get Inside Your Character's Head

Now try getting even further inside your character's head. Think about the saying "Actions speak louder than words." Ask yourself how your character would act in different situations. This will help you dig even deeper into your character's true self and reveal some of your character's secrets.

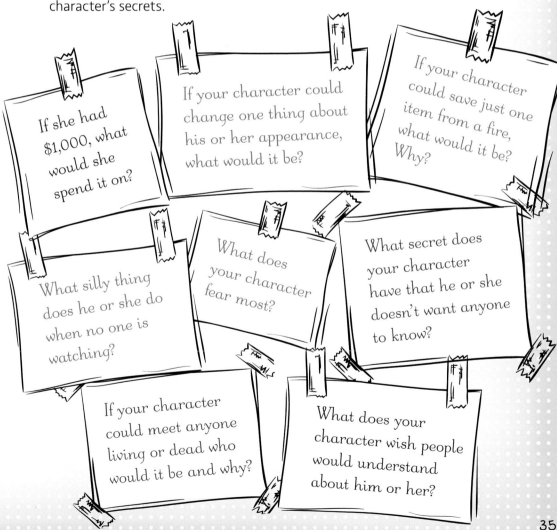

If she had $1,000, what would she spend it on?

If your character could change one thing about his or her appearance, what would it be?

If your character could save just one item from a fire, what would it be? Why?

What silly thing does he or she do when no one is watching?

What does your character fear most?

What secret does your character have that he or she doesn't want anyone to know?

If your character could meet anyone living or dead who would it be and why?

What does your character wish people would understand about him or her?

Choose a picture of a person from an Internet image search and create a fictional character using the photo. First, list everything you can imagine about this person. What pictures are on his or her phone? What food will this person absolutely not eat and why? What's the person's happiest memory? Use your answers to write a story featuring your new character.

AUTHOR PROFILE:

Walter Dean Myers

Walter Dean Myers wrote more than 100 books for young people. He was awarded two Newbery honor medals for his work and served as the National Ambassador for Young People's Literature. *145th Street: Short Stories* is a collection of 10

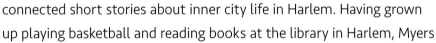

connected short stories about inner city life in Harlem. Having grown up playing basketball and reading books at the library in Harlem, Myers often set his stories there. Myers struggled in school, but a teacher saw promise in his writing. Even though he dropped out of school, Myers remembered his teacher's advice and wrote at night after work. In addition to fiction, Walter Dean Myers also wrote picture books and nonfiction. He died in 2014.

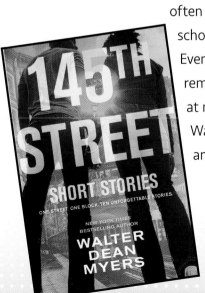

Chapter 5

Getting to the Point

Point of View

Have you ever argued with a friend? Perhaps you wondered why your friend couldn't see your side of things. People interpret events differently based on what they know and how it affects them. That's called point of view. In a story two characters can experience and view the same situation in different ways because their different backgrounds color how they interpret the same events. That's why your best friend may not always see things your way. When writing a story you have to choose which point of view you'll use to tell the story.

First Person

If you write as if the main character is narrating, or telling the story, you're using first person point of view. One clue to identifying first person point of view is the use of first person pronouns such as I, me, and my. Writing in first person gives readers a close, intimate view of a character's true nature.

Edgar Allen Poe uses first person point of view in his short story "The Tell-Tale Heart." In it a madman tells the story of a crime he commits. Notice the use of first-person pronouns and how the character speaks like a madman.

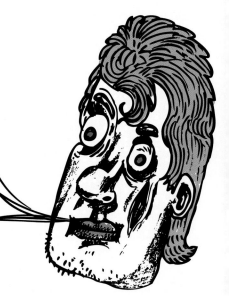

"True!—nervous—very, very dreadfully nervous I had been and am; but why will you say that I am mad? The disease had sharpened my senses—not destroyed—not dulled them. Above all was the sense of hearing acute. I heard all things in the heaven and in the earth. I heard many things in hell. How, then, am I mad? Hearken! And observe how healthily—how calmly I can tell you the whole story."

Third Person

When a narrator tells the story, you are using third person point of view. If your narrator only knows the actions being played out, it's called third person limited. If your narrator sees all and knows all, it's called third person omniscient point of view. Writing in third person gives readers a broad overview of things.

Jack London narrates his short story "In a Far Country" using a third person point of view. Notice how third person point of view is like a sports announcer telling what is happening.

"When the world rang with the tale of Arctic gold, and the lure of the North gripped the heartstrings of men, Carter Weatherbee threw up his snug clerkship, turned the half of his savings over to his wife, and with the remainder bought an outfit. . . . Like many another fool, disdaining the old trails used by the Northland pioneers for a score of years, he hurried to Edmonton in the spring of the year; and there, unluckily for his soul's welfare, he allied himself with a party of men."

Take a few paragraphs from a story and rewrite them from a different point of view. Start with the excerpts from "In a Far Country" and "The Tell-Tale Heart." As you rewrite "In a Far Country" in first person, get inside Carter Weatherbee's head. Tell his thoughts and hopes as he prepares for his trip to the Arctic. You'll likely find that changing the story to first person makes the reader feel closer to the main character. When you change "The Tell-Tale Heart" into third person point of view, you'll want to step outside of the madman's head a bit and narrate as an observer rather than the madman himself. Ask yourself whether the story is more interesting from the madman's point of view or the third person narrator's. Next, try experimenting with different points of view in the stories you write.

Theme

Most stories have a theme, or life lesson. The theme is often the point of the story, or the big idea the author wants the reader to understand. To figure out the theme, look at the root of the conflict and the ending. A story's title might hint at its theme as well. Stories rarely state the theme explicitly. Usually you have to put on your thinking cap to figure it out. Ask yourself what the main character has learned.

Getting to Know: Charles Dickens

In Charles Dickens' "A Christmas Carol," Ebenezer Scrooge is stingy and unkind to his workers, family, and friends until he is visited by three spirits who show him the fault of his stingy ways. The story's end shows us its theme, which might be expressed as—giving is good for the soul.

"He became as good a friend, as good a master, and as good a man, as the good old city knew. . . . Some people laughed to see the alteration in him, but he let them laugh. . . . His own heart laughed: and that was quite enough for him. . . . And it was always said of him, that he knew how to keep Christmas well, if any man alive possessed the knowledge. May that be truly said of us, and all of us! And so, as Tiny Tim observed, God bless us, every one!"

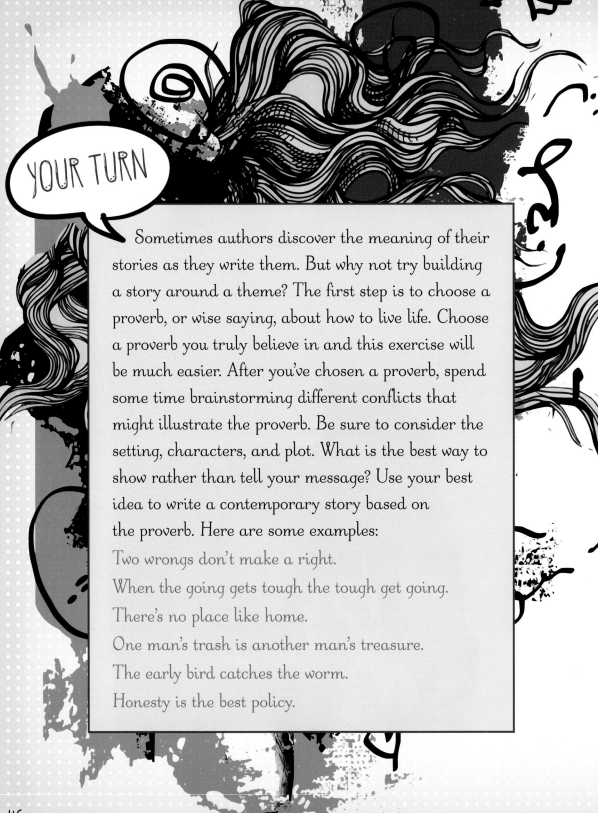

YOUR TURN

   Sometimes authors discover the meaning of their stories as they write them. But why not try building a story around a theme? The first step is to choose a proverb, or wise saying, about how to live life. Choose a proverb you truly believe in and this exercise will be much easier. After you've chosen a proverb, spend some time brainstorming different conflicts that might illustrate the proverb. Be sure to consider the setting, characters, and plot. What is the best way to show rather than tell your message? Use your best idea to write a contemporary story based on the proverb. Here are some examples:

Two wrongs don't make a right.

When the going gets tough the tough get going.

There's no place like home.

One man's trash is another man's treasure.

The early bird catches the worm.

Honesty is the best policy.

AUTHOR PROFILE:

Agatha Christie

Best known for creating the amateur sleuth Miss Marple and the retired detective Hercule Poirot, Agatha Christie didn't set out to become one of the most famous female writers. Following World War I (1914–1918) young Agatha began working in a pharmacy giving out medication. Though she was good at her job, she found the work boring. Boredom and a dare from her sister led Christie to take up her pen. She wrote her first detective story "The Mysterious Affair at Styles" starring Belgian detective Hercule Poirot. But her pharmaceutical background came in very handy when killing off characters with poison. In fact, her descriptions of poisonings were so convincing that her stories even got reviews in pharmacy magazines! Agatha Christie often found inspiration in children's nursery rhymes, which is evident in some of her stories' titles, such as "How Does your Garden Grow?" and "Four and Twenty Blackbirds."

Chapter 6

Special Techniques

A great plot, conflict, and well-developed characters will take you far in writing a short story. But seasoned writers have a few more tricks up their sleeves.

Foreshadowing

Remember the story of Hansel and Gretel? Hansel left a trail of bread crumbs so he and his sister could find their way home. Believe it or not, authors often leave a trail of clues or hints to help the reader find her way to the story's solution. This is called foreshadowing. Foreshadowing often calls the reader's attention to an object or action that will later be important in the story. You've probably experienced foreshadowing if you've ever been able to solve a book's mystery or problem before the ending.

Getting to Know: Edgar Allan Poe

Edgar Allan Poe hints at the twisted ending of "The Cask of Amantillado" with foreshadowing. The narrator wants revenge, so he lures Fortunato to a deep underground crypt with plans to seal him inside. In order to lead Fortunato to his doom, the narrator must first gain his trust. Notice how Poe points out that trust at the beginning of the story to foreshadow Fortunato's death, or "immolation," at the narrator's hands.

> "It must be understood, that neither by word nor deed had I given Fortunato cause to doubt my good will. I continued, as was my wont, to smile in his face, and he did not perceive that my smile now was at the thought of his immolation."

Later in the story, Fortunato breaks into a coughing spell. The narrator fakes concern for Fortunato, but Fortunato insists, "The cough is a mere nothing; it will not kill me. I shall not die of a cough." The narrator replies, "True — true." This is strong foreshadowing. It is beginning to become clear that Fortunato won't die of his cough, but he will die of something!

Think about the ending of a story you want to write. Hint at the ending of your story by planting relevant objects or actions earlier in your story. For example, a story that climaxes in a dangerous mountain climb might foreshadow this event by sprinkling mentions of rope, hiking shoes, dangerous conditions, or falling rocks throughout the story.

Plot Twists

Sometimes you want to let the reader in on the action early in the story by foreshadowing. Other times you want to keep your reader guessing right to the end. When you lead your reader down one road, and then take a sudden, surprising turn in another direction, that's called a plot twist. If you've ever read a book or seen a movie and thought "I didn't see that coming!" then you've experienced a plot twist. O. Henry was the master of the plot twist. He always had something up his sleeve that the reader didn't expect.

Getting to Know: O. Henry

In his short story "After Twenty Years," O. Henry describes an appointment two friends make to meet in the same spot 20 years later. Bob shows up first. While waiting for his long-lost old friend, Jimmy, to arrive, he strikes up a conversation with a police officer. Just as the reader feels convinced the police officer is Jimmy, the officer leaves and a few minutes later a new man shows up claiming to be Jimmy.

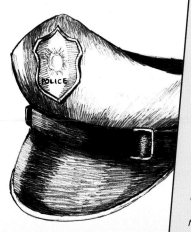

"At the corner stood a drug store, brilliant with electric lights. When they came into the glare each of them turned simultaneously to gaze upon the other's face.

"The man from the West stopped suddenly and released his arm.

"'You're not Jimmy Wells,' he snapped. 'Twenty years is a long time, but not long enough to change a man's nose from a Roman to a pug.'

"'It sometimes changes a good man into a bad one,'" said the tall man. 'You've been under arrest for ten minutes, "Silky" Bob. Chicago thinks you may have dropped over our way and wires us she wants to have a chat with you. Going quietly, are you? That's sensible. Now, before we go to the station here's a note I was asked to hand to you. You may read it here at the window. It's from Patrolman Wells.'

"'Bob: I was at the appointed place on time. When you struck the match to light your cigar I saw it was the face of the man wanted in Chicago. Somehow I couldn't do it myself, so I went around and got a plain clothes man to do the job. JIMMY.'"

Try your hand at planning a plot twist. To successfully use this writing technique, it's helpful to plan out the plot before you begin writing. First decide how you'll surprise your readers. Will the hero and villain switch roles? Will solving one difficult conflict create a new, bigger conflict? Will one of the main characters die unexpectedly? Planning the twist ahead of time allows you to drop tiny hints, clues, or distractions in the narrative leading up to the plot twist.

No matter how you decide to twist the plot, it's important to keep readers' reactions in mind. Readers may feel angry if the story tricks or misleads them in an unbelievable or disappointing way. Plan out all the details well before you begin writing to be sure the twist feels unexpected, but also believable—or, better yet, inevitable!

Figurative Language

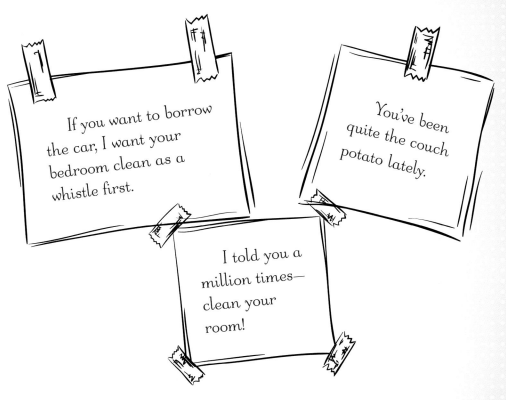

If you want to borrow the car, I want your bedroom clean as a whistle first.

You've been quite the couch potato lately.

I told you a million times—clean your room!

Sometimes language is not intended to be taken literally, or word for word. Instead it expresses an imaginative description or comparison, or figurative language.

Think of figurative language as the seasoning you add to your writing. Shake a little figurative language into your writing, but don't dump in too much. Treat figurative language in a story like you'd treat salt in a recipe. A pinch of salt adds flavor, but a cup of salt ruins the soup. Two kinds of figurative language you can add into your writing are similes and metaphors.

Simile

A simile compares two things using the word "like" or the word "as." Similes show how one thing is similar to another. Here are two examples from Sir Arthur Conan Doyle's first Sherlock Holmes story, "A Study in Scarlet."

Watson describes a man who considers himself a detective:

"This amateur bloodhound caroled away like a lark while I meditated upon the many-sidedness of the human mind."

The amateur detective tells Sherlock Holmes he has solved the mystery:

"I have made the whole thing as clear as day."

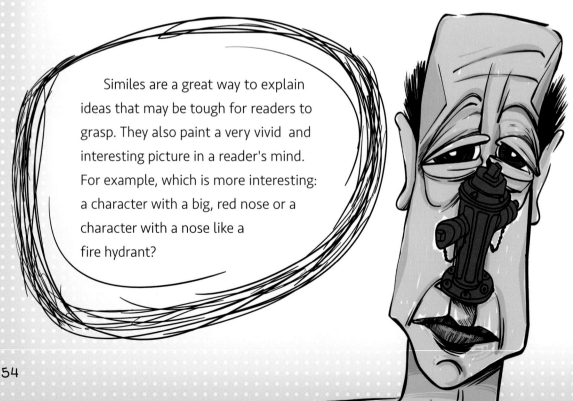

Similes are a great way to explain ideas that may be tough for readers to grasp. They also paint a very vivid and interesting picture in a reader's mind. For example, which is more interesting: a character with a big, red nose or a character with a nose like a fire hydrant?

Metaphor

A metaphor compares two things by stating one thing is something else. Unlike its cousin the simile, a metaphor doesn't use any signal words such as "like." Take a look at these metaphors.

A character describing Sherlock Holmes says,

"You'll find him a knotty problem, though."

Sherlock Holmes quotes his own writing to Watson:

"So all life is a great chain, the nature of which is known whenever we are shown a single link of it."

Watson responds without knowing Holmes was the author:

"I never read such rubbish in my life."

Holmes descibes his crime-solving work with Watson:

"There's the scarlet thread of murder running through the colorless skein of life, and our duty is to unravel it, and isolate it, and expose every inch of it."

Both metaphors and similes can make powerful comparisons and visual images. They are both great tools for your writing. So how do you chose which one to use?

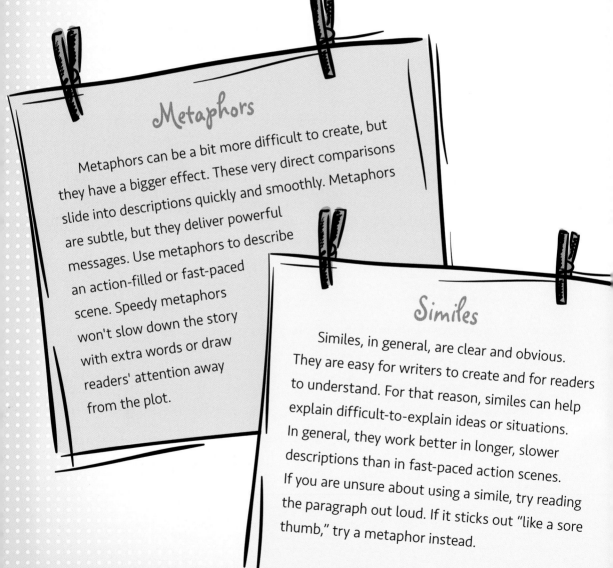

Metaphors

Metaphors can be a bit more difficult to create, but they have a bigger effect. These very direct comparisons slide into descriptions quickly and smoothly. Metaphors are subtle, but they deliver powerful messages. Use metaphors to describe an action-filled or fast-paced scene. Speedy metaphors won't slow down the story with extra words or draw readers' attention away from the plot.

Similes

Similes, in general, are clear and obvious. They are easy for writers to create and for readers to understand. For that reason, similes can help explain difficult-to-explain ideas or situations. In general, they work better in longer, slower descriptions than in fast-paced action scenes. If you are unsure about using a simile, try reading the paragraph out loud. If it sticks out "like a sore thumb," try a metaphor instead.

YOUR TURN

Write a scene using at least one simile and one metaphor. One way to incorporate a simile is to use it to describe a character. For example, you could write she's as _____ as a _____. An easy way to create a metaphor is to start with a simile, then take away the "like" or "as." For example, if you write the simile "she's as delicate as a daisy" just rewrite it and omit "as" and you get "She's a delicate daisy," which is a metaphor. Easy peasy!

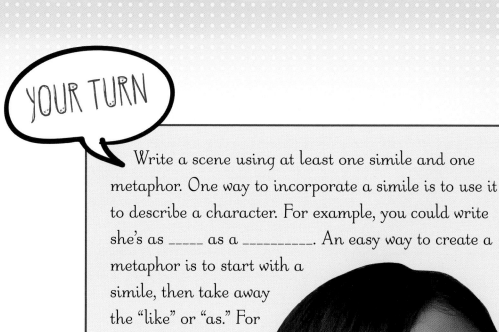

Keep It Fresh

It's fun and inspirational to try out new writing techniques. But wait—have you ever heard the saying "Know thyself?" Another excellent way to improve your writing is to take a close look at what you already know and practice!

Grab a couple samples of your writing, or, if possible, completed stories that you have written. Now imagine you are reading your work for the very first time. Sometimes it helps to read it out loud—especially if you don't normally do so. As you read, keep your eyes and ears open for quirks, habits, and repetition. Do you use one particular word over and over? Use an online thesaurus to look up synonyms for those poor, repeated, overworked words! Do you end every other sentence with an exclamation point? Make sure only the sentences that are truly *exclaimed* get this exceptional punctuation.

On the other hand, if every sentence ends in a period, why not break it up with an occasional question? Remember to vary your sentence structure and length too. Work to create sentences and paragraphs that you can read with a natural rhythm and without stumbling. Like a great new haircut or outfit, change is good! By "knowing thyself," including thy writing habits, you will find even more ways to grow as a writer.

YOUR TURN

You might think that the shorter the story, the easier it will be to write. But that's not necessarily so! Want to test it out? For this writing exercise, try writing a ultra-short story. Limit your entire story to 200, 150, or even 100 words. Remember, even ultra-short stories need to have essential story elements. The characters and situations should feel real and full, and the plot must have a beginning, middle, and end.

Ultra-shorts force you to use crisp, precise language—no thoughtless repetition. When you have a word limit, each word becomes more important. But remember, no matter what you are writing, conciously choosing the best, freshest words possible is always a good practice!

"The difference between the right word and the almost right word is the difference between lightning and a lightning bug."

-Mark Twain, *The Wit and Wisdom of Mark Twain*

Chapter 7

Conclusion

Completing a short story is a rewarding experience. Just think, you can say you created something out of nothing! New worlds, new characters, and new experiences came into being just because you imagined them and wrote them down.

Even if one of your stories doesn't turn out as well as you planned, remember that you're learning through practice. Give yourself permission to make mistakes and learn from them. Plus, no story has to be perfect on the first attempt. Through revision, feedback from trusted friends, and practice, each draft will hone your skills.

With every story you write, you'll get better at your craft and feel more confident in your abilities. You don't have to publish a story to live the creative life of a writer. All you have to do is pick up your pen and paper and get started!

Works Cited

Bradbury, Ray. *Bradbury Stories: 100 of His Most Celebrated Tales.* New York: William Morrow, 2003.

Christie, Agatha, and Charles Todd. *Hercule Poirot: The Complete Short Stories.* New York: William Morrow, 2013.

Dickens, Charles, and Mark Peppe. *A Christmas Carol.* [New] ed. London: Puffin, 2008.

Henry, O. *Best Short Stories.* Mineola, N.Y.: Dover Publications, 2002.

Irving, Washington. *The Legend of Sleepy Hollow and Other Stories.* Mineola, N.Y.: Dover, 2008.

Kipling, Rudyard. *A Collection of Rudyard Kipling's Just So Stories.* Cambridge, MA: Candlewick Press, 2004.

London, Jack, and Robert Court. *Jack London: Collected Short Stories.* Mankato, Minn.: Peterson Pub., 2002.

Poe, Edgar Allan, and Neil Gaiman. *Selected Poems & Tales.* New York: Barnes & Noble, 2004.

Twain, Mark. *The Complete Short Stories.* New York: Alfred A. Knopf, 2012.

Glossary

characterization (kar-ik-tuhr-i-ZA-shen)—the act of describing the qualities of someone

climax (KLYE-maks)—the most exciting or intense part of a story

conflict (CON-flict)—the problem faced in a story

foreshadow (for-SHAD-o)—to hint at what's to come

metaphor (MET-uh-FOR)—figure of speech that paints a word picture; calling a man "a mouse" is a metaphor from which we learn in one word that the man is timid or weak, not that he is actually a mouse

narrator (na-RATE-or)—the person who tells a story or describes an event

plot—sequence of events that drives a story forward; the problems that the hero must resolve

plot twist—an unexpected turn of events that changes the expected course of the story

point of view—eyes through which the story is told

setting—the time and place of a story

simile (SIM-uh-lee)—a figure of speech that compares different things using the words "like" or "as"

theme (THEEM)—main idea that the story addresses, such as good versus evil or the importance of truth; a story can have more than one theme

Read More

Benke, Karen. *Rip the Page!: Adventures in Creative Writing.* Boston: Trumpeter, 2010.

Llanas, Sheila Griffin. *Picture Yourself Writing Fiction: Using Photos to Inspire Writing.* Capstone Press, 2012.

Mazer, Anne, and Ellen Potter. *Spilling Ink: A Young Writer's Handbook.* New York: RB Flash Point/Roaring Brook Press, 2010.

Internet Sites

Use FactHound to find Internet sites related to this book.
All of the sites on FactHound have been researched by our staff.

Here's all you do:

Visit *www.facthound.com*

Type in this code: **9781491459911**

Index

About the Author

Rebecca Langston-George is the author of several books including *Choice Words: A Crash Course in Language Arts*; *A Primary Source History of the Dust Bowl*; and *For the Right to Learn: The Malala Yousafzai Story*. She's a middle school language arts teacher and the Assistant Regional Advisor for the Society of Children's Writers and Illustrators in Central-Coastal California.